Carlo Scarpa

Casa Veritti
Casa Ottolenghi

Residential Masterpieces 08
Carlo Scarpa
Casa Veritti
Casa Ottolenghi

Text by Yoshio Futagawa
Edited and photographed by Yukio Futagawa
Art direction: Gan Hosoya

Copyright © 2010 A.D.A. EDITA Tokyo Co., Ltd.
3-12-14 Sendagaya, Shibuya-ku, Tokyo 151-0051, Japan
All rights reserved. No part of this publication may be reproduced,
stored in a retrieval system, or transmitted,
in any form or by any means, electronic, mechanical,
photocopying, recording, or otherwise,
without permission in writing from the publisher.

Copyright of photographs
©2010 GA photographers

Printed and bound in Japan

ISBN 978-4-87140-633-8 C1352

Residential Masterpieces 08

Carlo Scarpa

Casa Veritti
Udine, Italy, 1955-61

Casa Ottolenghi
Bardolino, Italy, 1974-79

Text by Yoshio Futagawa

Edited and Photographed by Yukio Futagawa

世界現代住宅全集08
カルロ・スカルパ
ヴェリッティ邸
イタリア，ウディネ　1955-61
オットーレンギ邸
イタリア，バルドリーノ　1974-79
文：二川由夫
企画・編集・撮影：二川幸夫

ディテールの「洪水」――二川由夫
'Deluge' of Detail *by Yoshio Futagawa*

ここに紹介する二軒の住宅は，イタリア国内のみならず20世紀の住宅建築史において最高峰のクオリティを持った名作建築である。二軒の住宅はそれらが手掛けられた時期に約20年の隔たりがあり，その作風は異なるものの，この建築家の作家人生において重要な二つのマイルストーンとして輝き，今なおその素晴らしい姿とそこに展開する空間体験は，現代の我々に建築が本来持つ創造の深さとは何かを訴えかけているかのようである。

20世紀イタリア建築界の巨匠＝カルロ・スカルパ。1906年ヴェネチアに生まれ，20歳の時，ヴェネチア美術学校の建築学科を卒業し，同大学の助手となる。以降，大学での教鞭は建築家の創作活動とともに彼のライフワークの一翼であり，「プロフェッソール」の肩書きは「マエストロ」とともに彼を表すもう一つの呼称であった。

戦前，初期の仕事には建築プロジェクトは少なく，代わりにヴェネチア，ムラノ島の伝統工芸であるガラス器のデザインを多く手掛けている。その卓越したデザイナーの詩的な感性と職人達の伝統的な高い技術の協働の結晶である作品には，スカルパ独自の美の世界がつくり上げられ，彼を一流の工芸デザイナーとして有名にした。職人達の持つ高い技術力や，古今・多彩な素材や技法による工芸的なクオリティは，彼が展開した新しい建築にも積極的に取り込まれ，独特な建築世界を展開することになる。それはやがて，建築と工芸，インダストリアル・デザインなどといった，細分化される創作のジャンルを超えた存在に登り詰めることになる。

「ヴェリッティ邸」
スカルパは，フランク・ロイド・ライトの建築を共に研究をしていたアンジェロ・マジエリの親戚であるルイジ・ヴェリッティ弁護士から住宅設計の依頼を受けることとなった。ウディネの街中にある敷地はいわゆる旗竿形であり，それは大通りから車一台が通れる程の幅の長いアプローチがその奥の方形の敷地の端に到達するというものであった。

この住宅が，この敷地のアプローチの作る軸線に対して平行なグリッドとそれから45度傾けられた二次的なグリッド，そしてオーバーラップされる円を基準として設計されていることに，フランク・ロイド・ライトの典型的な設計手法との類似性が見られる。加えてファサードを飾るコンクリートブロックの柱に与えられた装飾や開口部，木製サッシの窓割り，手すりの支柱に塗られる鮮やかな中華風の朱色などにも，ライト風のディテールが多く見られ，当時のスカルパが如何にライトに多大な影響を受けていたかを物語っている。ライトの影響は，スカルパにとって，この住宅を手がける以前に遡る時期に傾倒していた，ウィーン世紀末のヨーゼフ・ホフマンなどが展開した分離

The two houses introduced here are masterpieces with the highest quality not only within Italy but also in the history of 20th century residential architecture. Despite the presence of a gap of twenty years between the periods of their creation and a difference in their respective styles, these two houses are important milestones that illuminate this architect's life as an artist. Their glorious figure and spatial experience provided there never cease to appeal to our generation today in terms of the depth of creation that is innate to architecture.

Carlo Scarpa, master of 20th-century Italian architecture, was born in Venice in 1906. He graduated the architectural department of Academy of Fine Arts at the age of 20 and became assistant professor at the Academy. Subsequently, his teaching at the Academy became a part of his lifework along his creative practice as architect. He has been called by his title 'Professor' as well as 'Maestro.'

Prior to WWII, his earlier works consisted mainly of glassware design, a traditional craft of Murano, Venice, instead of architectural projects. They were the product of collaboration between the poetic sensitivity of an extraordinary designer and the high level of traditional technology of craftsmen, that represent Scarpa's own world of beauty, and gained him fame as a top crafts designer. He was eager to incorporate the craftsmen's high level of technology and quality realized through various methods and materials old and new to his architecture and came to develop an architectural world of his own. In the course of time, his art worked its way up to become a presence that transcends segmentalized creative genres such as architecture, crafts and industrial design.

CASA VERITTI
Scarpa was offered a commission of house design from lawyer Luigi Veritti, a relative of Angelo Masieri with whom he has studied the architecture of Frank Lloyd Wright. Located in the city of Udine, the site has a flagpole shape with a long driveway off the main street wide enough for one car that reaches the edge of the rectangular site at its end.

The fact that this house has been designed based upon a grid parallel to the axis represented by the site's driveway, a secondary grid with a 45-degree inclination and overlapping circle, reveals a similarity to the design method typical of Frank Lloyd Wright. Additionally, ornaments and apertures on the concrete block columns decorating the facade, fenestration with wooden sash, and handrail posts colored with bright, Chinese-style vermillion are details that are reminiscent of Wright, demonstrating the magnitude of Wright's influence on Scarpa at the time. For Scarpa, Wright's influence was something associated with the decorative Secessionist architecture developed by Josef Hoffman in turn-of-the-century Vienna, in which he had been much involved before he began working on this residence. It looks as if

派の装飾的な建築と結び付いたものである。イタリア／ヨーロッパの伝統的な建築空間，装飾，そして施主の暮らし方にまで至る保守的な様式性とすり合わされた現代建築の有り様について，ライトの住宅建築が持っていたアメリカ流のフォーマル／カジュアルの二義的な方法論に可能性を見い出し，その手法を下敷きにしているかのようである。

道路からのアプローチで最初に出会う住宅は，敷地に対して45度に振られた面のファサードである。コンクリート・ブロックの重層による一対の柱，サンルームの木製サッシュとその上にそびえる煙突が強調する垂直のエレメントに縁取られ，古典的でフォーマルな表情が与えられている。しかしこの表情は，訪問者が住宅の周囲を移動することで変化してく。45度に振られたヴォリュームの重層は，立面を構成する同じエレメントが，見る位置によって新しい表情をつくり，最初に体験される正面性を和らげていく。玄関の軸線から見る立面のコンポジション，背部にある温室の低いヴォリューム，そして円形のプールの上に迫り出したガラス壁によって軽快感が与えられたサンルームの表情などは，それぞれカジュアルなものであり，フォーマルな印象は田園的に変化する。

あたかも浮いたような彫刻的な階段を3段上り，プールの端に掛けられたブリッジを渡ると玄関に至る。石張りの床を持つ玄関ホールは硬質な空間でフォーマルな性格が与えられている。その先の居間には木製の床が広がり，天井は比較的低く抑えられているも，隣接する2層吹き抜けのサンルームからの十分な自然光を受け，明るい空間となっている。ライト風に低い位置につくり付けられた様々な形の木製棚，壁というよりも家具の様に独立性の強い木製パーティション，マッシブな量感を持つ暖炉といったエレメントがこの空間を飾り，それらは総体として一つの美しい空間を調停するものである。

居間に隣接したサンルームは開放的な空間である。2層高さのガラス壁を2辺に持つ三角形の空間は，階段室の背部の吹き抜けと同様に上部の家族室と1階の空間を結ぶ役目も負うものでもあり，天井高の低い水平性の強い居間の空間に閉塞感を与えないものである。

食堂は基本的にフォーマルな性格の空間であり，美しいプロポーションの木製の壁とそれに与えられた開口のディテールなど，この住宅全体に共有される穏やかで礼儀正しい佇まいが与えられているが，この静寂を破り艶やかに演出するかのように，天井には流れるような緑色の帯が貫通されている。

2階はプライベートな諸室が置かれている。それらの意匠には，1階よりもよりカジュアルな性格の様々なディテールが与えられていることに気づく。

階段を上ると家族室に出る。家族室は第2の居間として，また各寝室の前室としての空間である。つくり付けの木製家具は低く抑えられ，

he has recognized a potential in the American-type equivocal methodology of formal/casual seen in Wright's residential architectures, as an option for the contemporary architecture's mixing with Italian/European traditional conservative styles that involve architectural space, decoration and the clients' way of living, and has used such method as a base.

Approached from the road, the first glimpse of the house is a surface standing at a 45-degree angle to the site that is the facade. Framed within a pair of columns made of piled-up concrete blocks, the sunroom's wooden sash and the vertical element emphasized by the chimney towering on top, it is given a classic, formal expression which is bound to change as visitors to this house move around the building. Layers of volumes shifted at 45-degree angle and identical elements that make up the elevation surface account for different expressions when seen from different positions that soften the frontality experienced at the very beginning. Vertical composition perceived from the entrance's axis; low volume of the winter garden in the back; and expression of the sunroom with glazed walls that protrude over the round pool to create a sense of lightness, are each casual in aspect, while the formal impression changes in a pastoral manner.

Three steps up the sculpturesque stairs that seem to float in the air, a bridge over a corner of the pool leads to the entrance. The stone-floored entrance hall is formal in character with its space with a hard, solid feeling. Follows a bright living room with an expanse of wood floor, a ceiling kept relatively low, and sufficient natural lighting provided by the adjacent double-height sunroom. Elements such as wooden shelves of various forms fixed at low positions in Wright's style, wooden partition wall that is highly independent like a piece of furniture, and massive fireplace decorate this space and as a whole contribute to the reconciled beauty of this space.

Next to the living room is the sunroom. It is an expansive triangular space with two double-height glazed walls, which also assumes a role of connecting the upper-level family room and the ground-floor space in the same manner as the double-height space behind the staircase does, preventing the highly horizontal space under the living room's low ceiling from being enclosed.

The dining room is basically a space with formal character, with beautifully proportioned wooden walls and detailed apertures on them that account for the gentle and courteous manners that are shared throughout this house. However, the ceiling is cut through by a flowing belt of glossy green as an attempt to break this silence.

The first floor accommodates private rooms with designs that feature a variety of details of more casual properties compared to those on ground floor.

Up the stairs is the family room, which serves as a second

その流れるような水平性はくつろぎの空間を演出する。
　主寝室と家族室を仕切る壁面にはスライド式の戸が付けられたユニークな形状の開口が設けられている。主寝室に面したベランダに付けられた手すりはフラットバーと木製の丸棒によるもので，それらの材料同士が見事にインテグレートされ素晴らしいディテールが実現されている。また，子供部屋は壁面に沿って多様なディテールの木製家具がつくられている。
　それらのディテールの「洪水」はスカルパならではのものであり，古典的なものから近代に至る，建築意匠のヴォキャブラリーから離脱するような革新的なデザインが縦横無尽に展開している。
　影響を受けたライトが展開した形式的なデザインのシステムとは違う，自由で豊富なヴォキャブラリーのディテール・デザイン群が与えられる壁面，またはその空間を一つにつくり上げ，さらには建築全体をつくり出すデザイン・プロセスは——実際のプロセスは所謂建築的な空間が最初に創られていたに違いないのだが——あたかもディテールから全体に向かうかのような錯覚を覚える，ディテールの「洪水」である。

「オットーレンギ邸」
ヴェリッティ邸を手掛けてから19年，ヴェローナの北，ガルダ湖を望む美しい緑深い敷地に建つ，建築家晩年の名作である。この住宅の施主もヴェリッティ邸と同様，弁護士を生業にするオットーレンギ氏である。マエストロはこの住宅でもその手腕を十二分に揮って，誰も為し得ない孤高の住宅建築を創り出している。この頃のスカルパは，それまでのキャリアの中での様々な影響や試行が自身の手法としてすべて昇華され，いよいよ自由自在な創作活動をしている。それは時代の烙印を受けることのない永遠の傑作となった。
　敷地には高さ制限があり，地形より高い建物を建てることが不可能であった。しかし，この制限がこの住宅を特徴的なものに仕立て上げる原動力の一つになっている。住宅は地形に埋め込まれる形で配置されたため，その平面は不定形であり，設計は地形との対話であったことが想像される。
　訪問者は，敷地より高い位置にある道路の，質素な鉄製ゲートからコンクリートの階段を下り，次に建物と擁壁の間に設けられた幅の狭い通路を進み，玄関に至ることになる。
　夫妻のための内部空間——居間，食堂，台所，書斎といった諸室はどこに居てもすべての気配を感じることのできる様な一室の空間として扱われて，この住宅のカジュアルな性格を決定している。高低差の与えられた各エリアはランドスケープのように扱われ，暖炉や収納となる低いパーティション・ヴォリュームで緩やかに仕切られて，空間全

living room as well as an anteroom for the bedrooms. The built-in wooden furniture is kept low in height as its fluid horizontality creates a space of comfort.

The wall between the master bedroom and the family room features a unique type of aperture with sliding doors. Handrails for the master bedroom balcony consists of flat bars and wooden round bars: different materials are skillfully integrated to realize this magnificent detail. Also, the child's room features a set of wooden furniture along its walls with a diversity of details.

The 'deluge' of such details is Scarpa's specialty, and is filled with a myriad of innovative designs that break away from the vocabulary of architectural design, from classic to modern.

His design process of assembling walls with details and designs of free, rich vocabulary that is different from the formal design system developed by Wright who was a source of his influence, to eventually create an entire architecture is—although the actual process must have started with creating the so-called architectural space—a 'deluge' of details that gives an impression as if the direction were from the details to the entirety.

CASA OTTOLENGHI
Built 19 years after Casa Veritti, this architect's later masterpiece is located on a site of lush green overlooking Lake Garda, north of Verona. Its client Ottolenghi is, like Veritti, a lawyer. For this house the maestro once again exercised his ability to create a residential architecture without equal like no one else could. At that time, Scarpa was freer than ever in his creative activities, with all of his influences and attempts in his career having been sublimed to a style of his own, that resulted in this immortal masterpiece that defies any labels of time.

The site being subject to height restriction, it was impossible to build anything taller than the land's peak. However, this restriction became one of the motivations for making this house a unique home. The house was embedded to fit the topography, hence the irregular shape of its floor plan. It is easy to imagine that its design consisted of dialogues with the topography.

Visitors to this house pass through the simple iron gate on the road above the site and take the concrete stairs down to a narrow approach between the building and the retaining wall that leads to the entrance.

The interior space for the couple accommodating such spaces as living room, dining room, kitchen is regarded as a large single space in which one can feel the presence of the other anywhere, defining the casual character of this house. Each area has different height and is treated as landscape. They are loosely partitioned by low volumes such as fireplace and storage to create a flowing relationship within the entire space. The ceiling over this singular space has a smooth surface finished with stucco, in a polyhedral shape that is like a reversed reproduction of the site's original topography. A mystic, cavernous at-

体には流れるような関係性がつくられている．この一室空間を覆う天井は，スタッコ仕上げの平滑な表面を持ち，形状は多面体であり，その様はあたかも敷地が元々持っていた地形を反転し再生したかの様であり，また，そこに映り込む光の揺らぎによって洞窟の様な神秘的な空間がつくり出されている．さらに，天井を支える円柱群は，コンクリートと大理石を層状に重ねたような意匠が与えられ，その量感は内部空間のアクセントとなっている．円柱と天井との境にはスタッコ・ワークによるスムーズなカーブによって天井に溶け込むようなディテールが与えられ，コンクリートの円柱はあたかも天井と接さずに自立して立っているような効果が生まれている．光沢のあるテラゾーの床には大柄な有機的模様が与えられて，この空間の詩的な性格を増幅し，建築的な規則性からさらに解き放つのに一役買っている．

主寝室は前述のパブリックな性格の一室空間から数段下ったレベルの奥に位置し，この住宅において最もプライベートな空間である．一室空間との境に置かれた円筒形のヴォリュームは浴室であり，寝室側の壁面に嵌め込まれたマジックミラーは室内の明るさの違いで鏡から窓に変化する．

内部空間に対して，外部に広がる庭は住宅のもう一つの主題である．庭はつくり込まずに自然な風景として用意されている．住宅の外壁は庭を彩るための背景でもあり，壁面に与えられているコンポジションはリバーシブルに内外の空間に向けて考慮されている．外部において庭を囲み込むように建つ壁面には蔦が絡まり，そのコンクリートの様々なテクスチャーは庭の自然との調和をもたらしている．建物の一翼に沿っておかれた池とそこに流れ込む水の音，塔状の煙突，その様相は古典建築の廃墟が自然に同化していくような詩的な風情を持ち，この住宅を時代を超越した名作に仕立て上げている．

住宅の各所には，スカルパ独特の金属，木，石，コンクリートなどの素材によるディテール・ワークがちりばめられている．

この住宅は従来のいかなる建築の形式やスタイルとも似ていない独特のものであり，この頃のスカルパが，自身の建築世界を完成させていたことを明らかに物語っている．それは単にスカルパの仕事の多くがイタリアの地方でつくられ，そのローカリティの環境に保護されていたためだけではなく，世界的なレベルの仕事であったことはマエストロの死後，多くのメディアに取り上げられるに従い，世界中の多くの建築家が影響を受けた事実を見れば明白である．

現代建築が見失っていた過去との接続，伝統的なクオリティの未来への昇華といった問題を，個人の作家として見事に一つの模範解答として示して見せたのだった．

mosphere is created by fluctuating light reflected upon the ceiling. A set of columns supporting the ceiling are designed as layers of concrete and marble, whose sense of mass gives an accent to the interior space. The border between the column and the ceiling is decorated with stucco work whose detail of smooth curve helps it merge into the ceiling, which is effective in making the concrete columns look as if they were standing on their own without touching the ceiling. A large, organic pattern is given to the lustrous terrazzo floor, as it plays a part in amplifying this space's poetic character and further release from architectural regularity.

The master bedroom is on a level several steps down from the aforementioned single space of public character, and is the most private space in the entire house. The cylindrical volume along the border of the single space is the bathroom. A one-way mirror is fixed to the wall on the bedroom side: it transforms from mirror to window due to the difference of room brightness.

In contrast with the interior space, the garden occupying the exterior is this house's another subject theme. Instead of being elaborate, it is prepared as natural landscape. The house's external wall is a background that adorns the garden, whose given composition is intended to be reversible toward both indoors and outdoors. The exterior features ivy-clad walls that surround the garden made of concrete of various textures that bring about harmony with nature in the garden. A pond arranged along a wing of the building, sound of water that flows into the pond and the towering chimney all make up a scenery with poetic flavor of ruins of classic architecture being absorbed by nature which succeeded in turning this house into a timeless masterpiece.

The entire house is sprinkled with detail works unique to Scarpa and various materials such as metal, wood, stone and concrete.

The distinctiveness of this residence looks like no other existing architectural forms and styles and clearly shows that Scarpa at the time has already perfected his own architectural world. It was possible not simply because many of Scarpa's works were executed in Italian provinces and have been protected by the environment of provincial locality, but because his works achieved world-level competency, which is especially evident from the fact that many architects around the world were eventually influenced by him as media coverage increased following the maestro's death.

As an individual artist he has successfully shown a model answer to the issues of sublimation of traditional qualities for the future and linkage with the past that contemporary architecture had lost.

English translation by Lisa Tani

Casa Veritti 1955-61

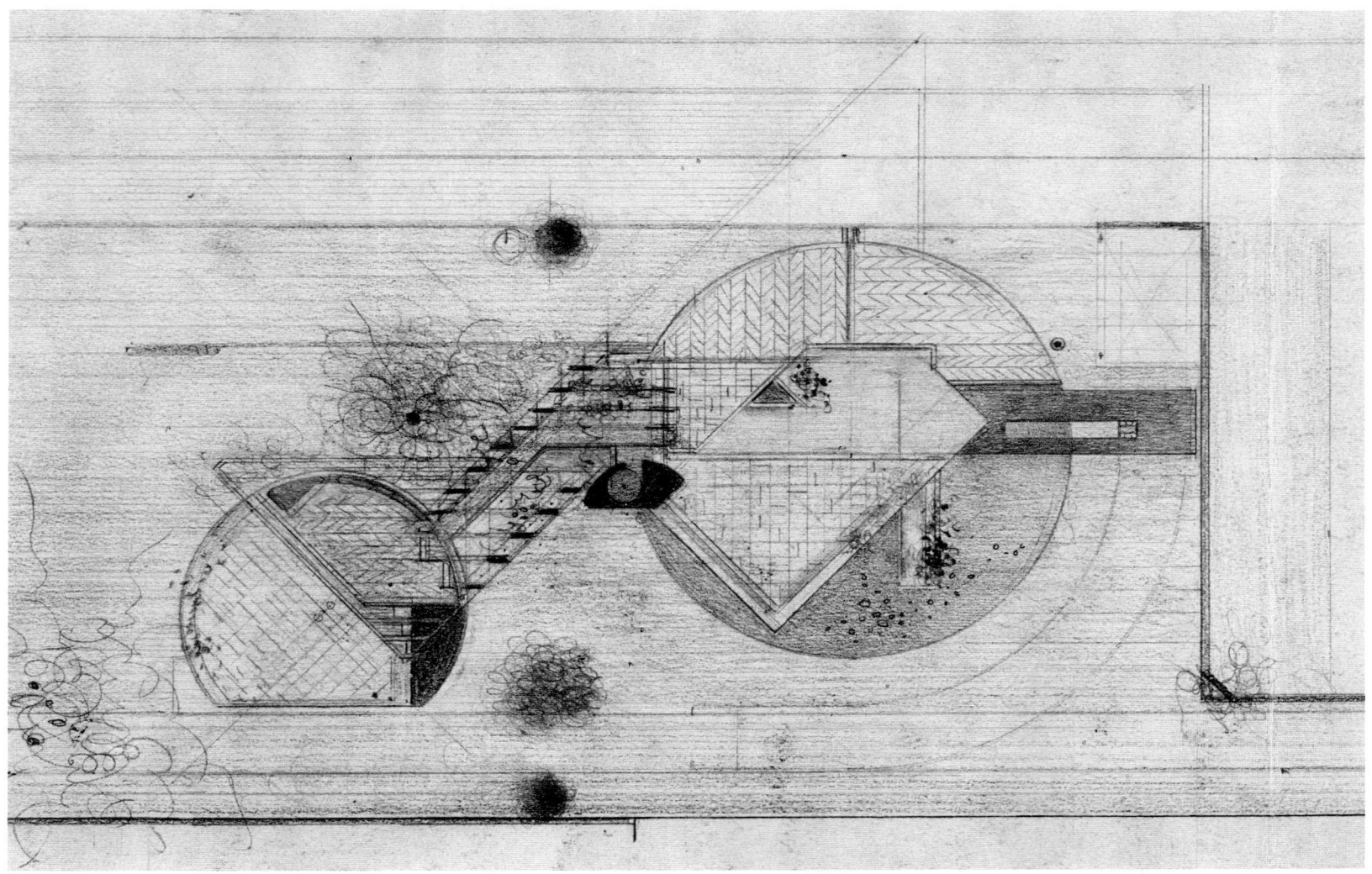

Plan (preliminary study)

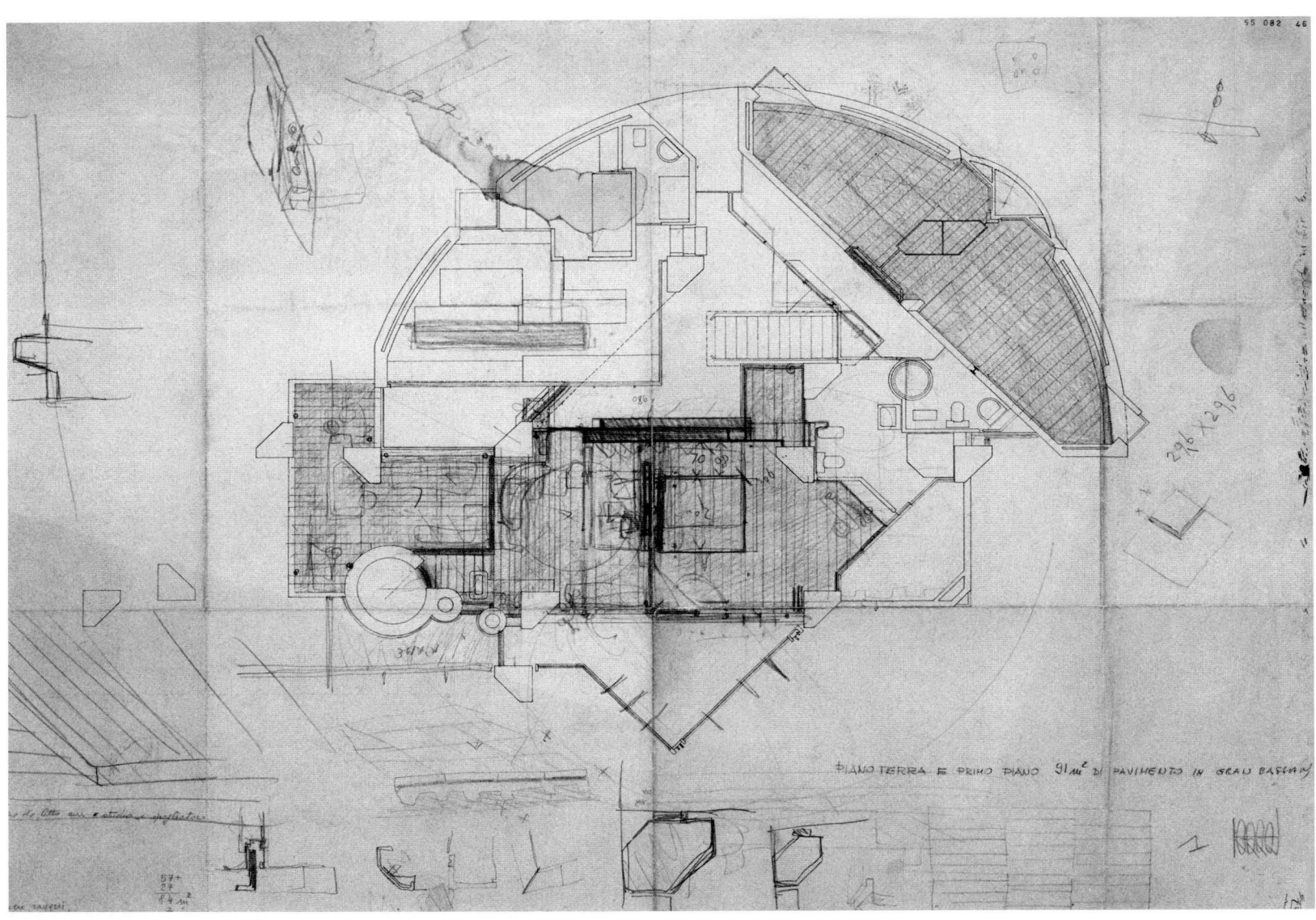
First floor

Approach:
view toward entrance from east. Pool on left

Pool facing living room

View toward house from garden

Greenhouse: view from south

Entrance hall: view toward living room

Staircase to first floor: view from entrance

Living room: dining room on right

Wooden sash of sunroom: sunshades on upper part, lattice window for ventilation

Sunroom at living room: glazed partitions on left are added later

Living room: view toward sunroom

Corner of living room: door to pool

Corner of living room: wooden fixture. Dining room on right

Wooden fixture at living room

Dining room

Void between living room (right) and dining room (left). Family room above

Dining room

Corner of family room on first floor. Void behind

Staircase: view from first floor

Family room on first floor

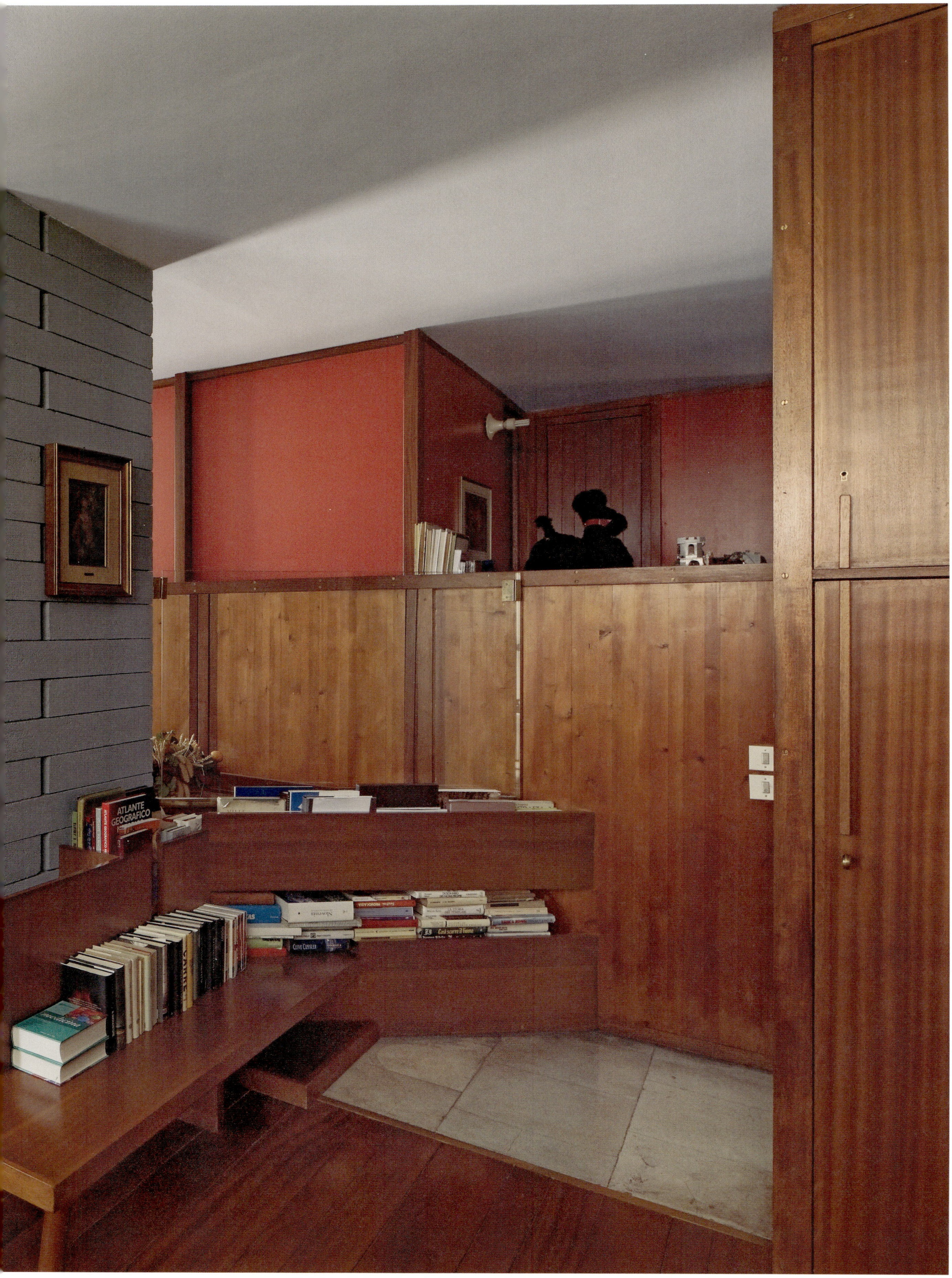
ATLANTE
GEOGRAFICO

Family room

Master bedroom on first floor: family room behind

Master bedroom: window is closed

Window is opened. Void of sunroom behind

Wooden doors of balcony

Spiral staircase at family room

Spiral staircase leading to roof terrace

Door to spiral staircase

Casa Ottolenghi 1974-79

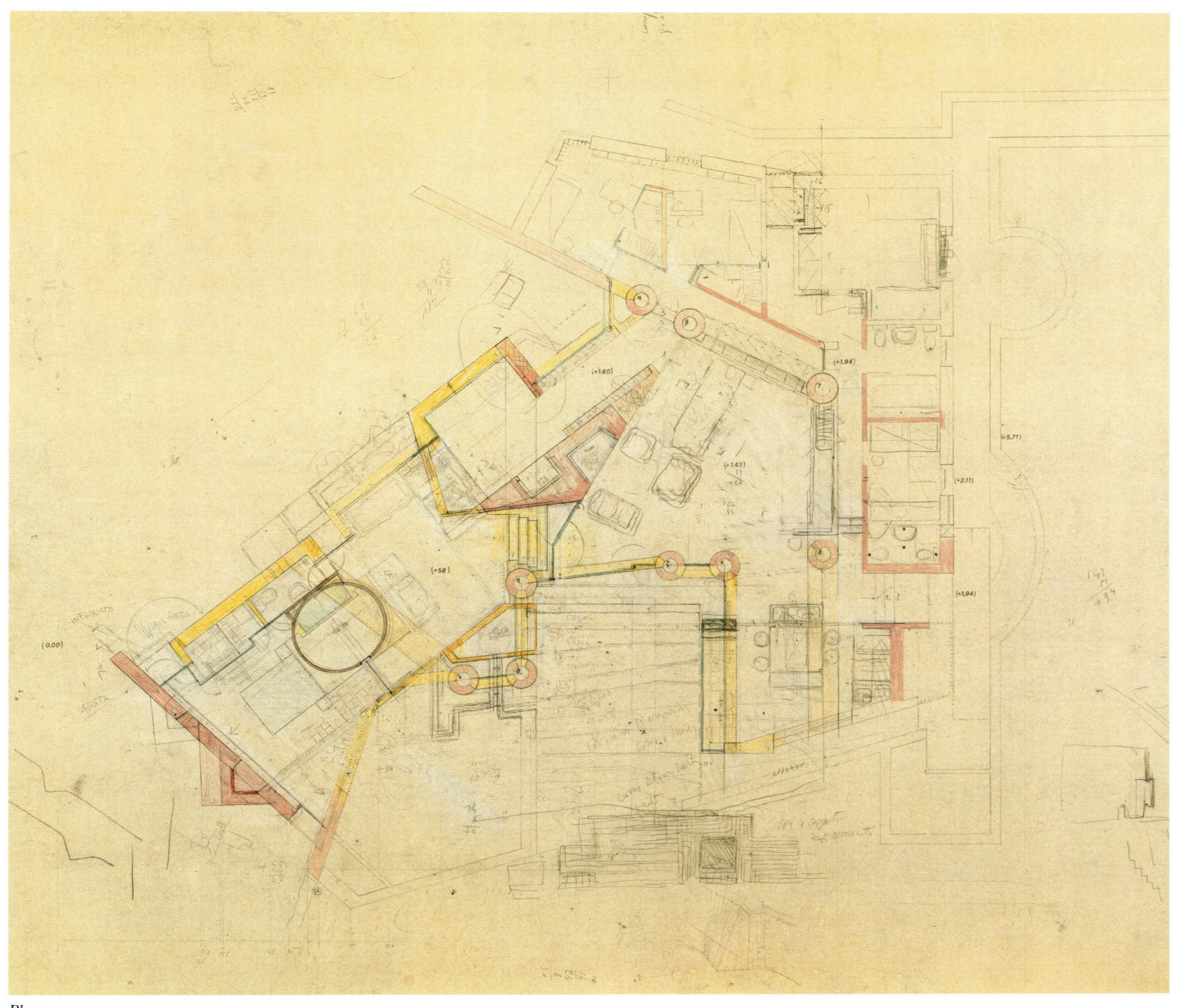

Plan

Approach

Entrance gate

Staircase from entrance gate

Staircase from entrance gate

Overall view toward Garda Lake

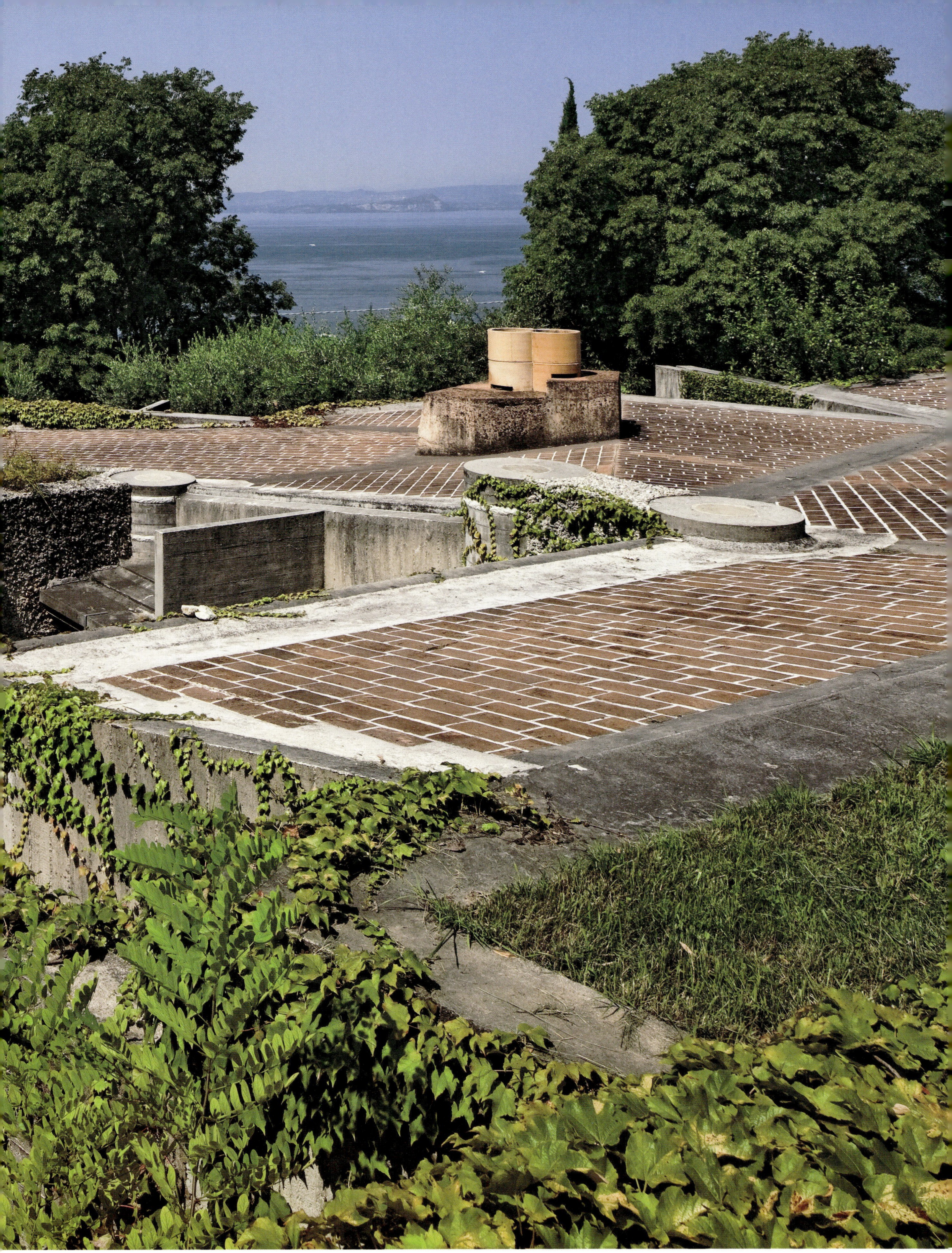

Passageway between gate and house

Downward view of passageway: entrance on left

Ivy on wall

View from garden. Chimney of master bedroom on left

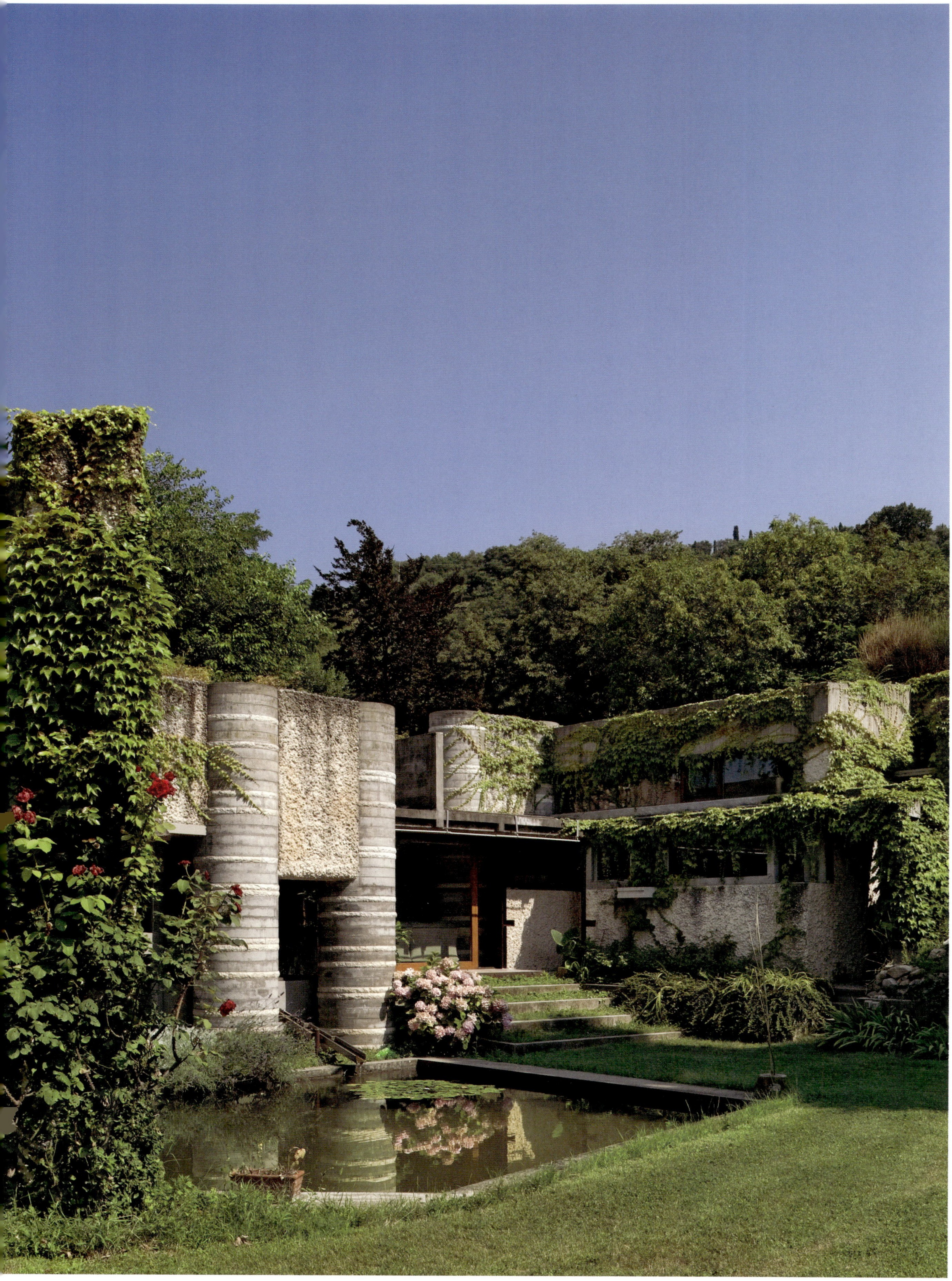

View from roof terrace toward garden

View toward garden from passageway

View toward living room from garden. Garden entrance on left

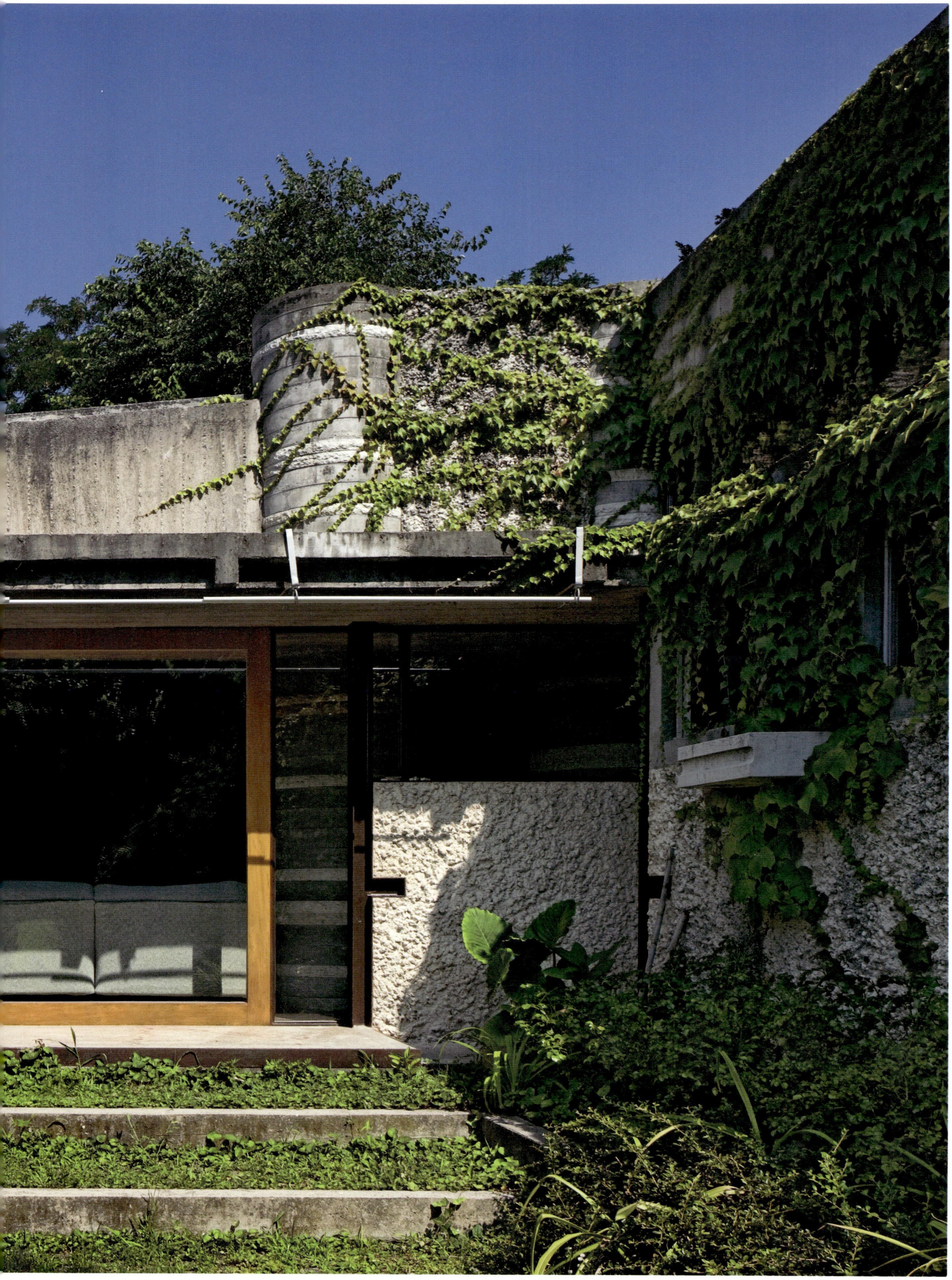

Garden facing living room

Garden: chimney of master bedroom on left

A pair of columns next to garden entrance

Living/dining room

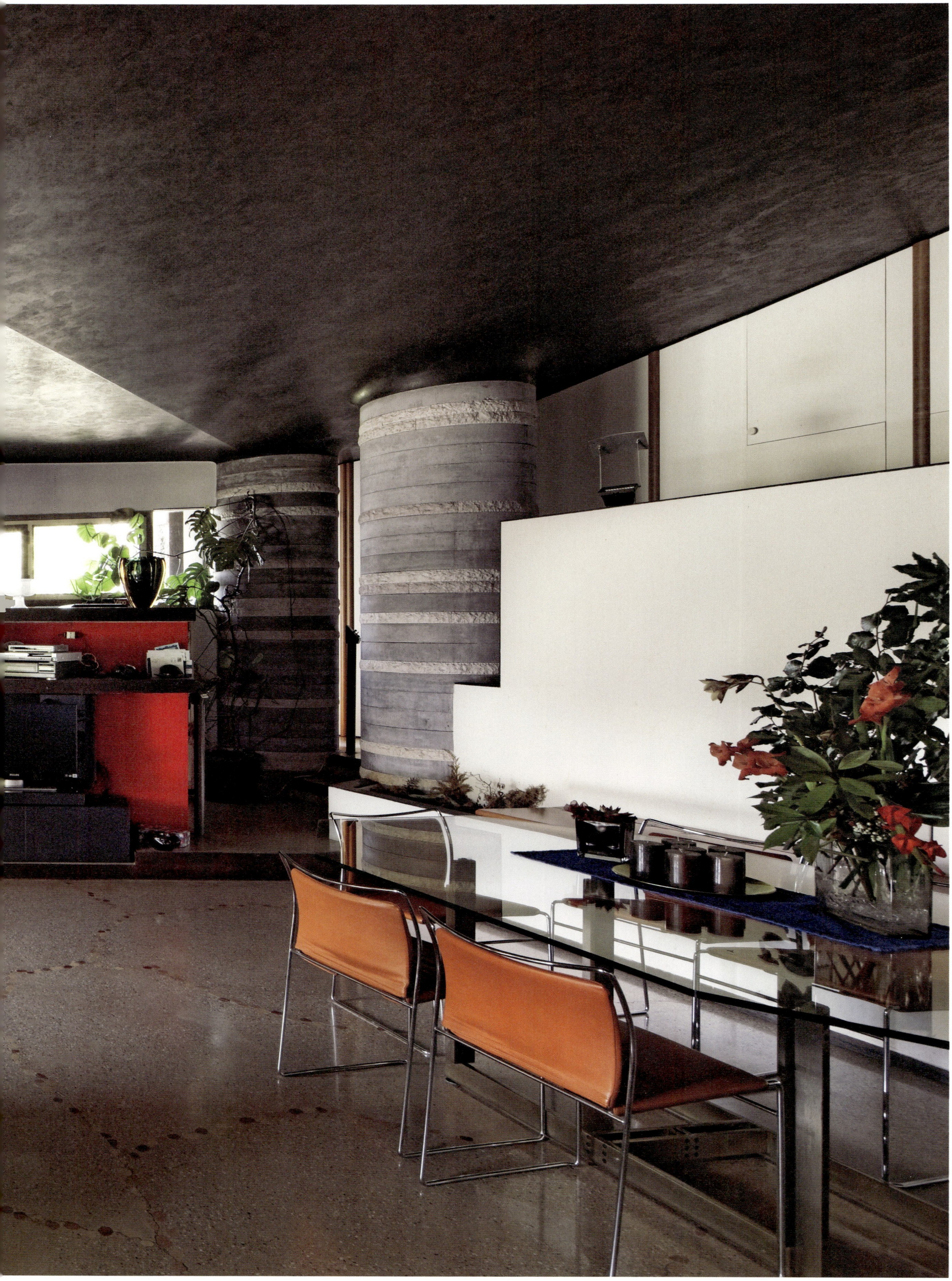

View toward garden from living room

Living room: kitchen on left

View toward garden and pool

Living room (photo of 1981: walls and ceilings were painted in different colours)

Living/dining room

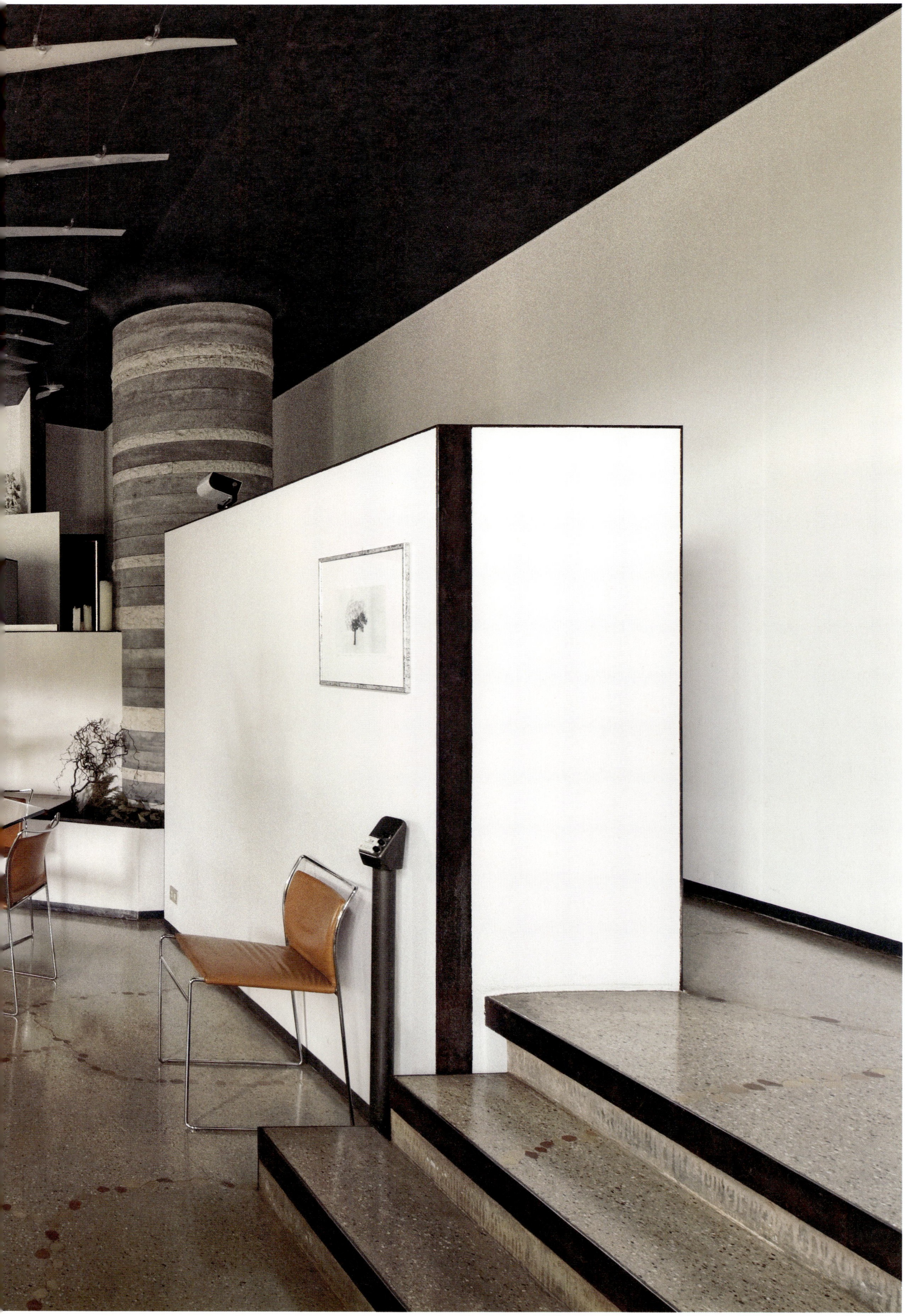

Corridor to bedrooms

Breakfast room

Kitchen windows

Kitchen

Breakfast room: kitchen behind

Staircase between master bedroom and living room (photo of 1981)

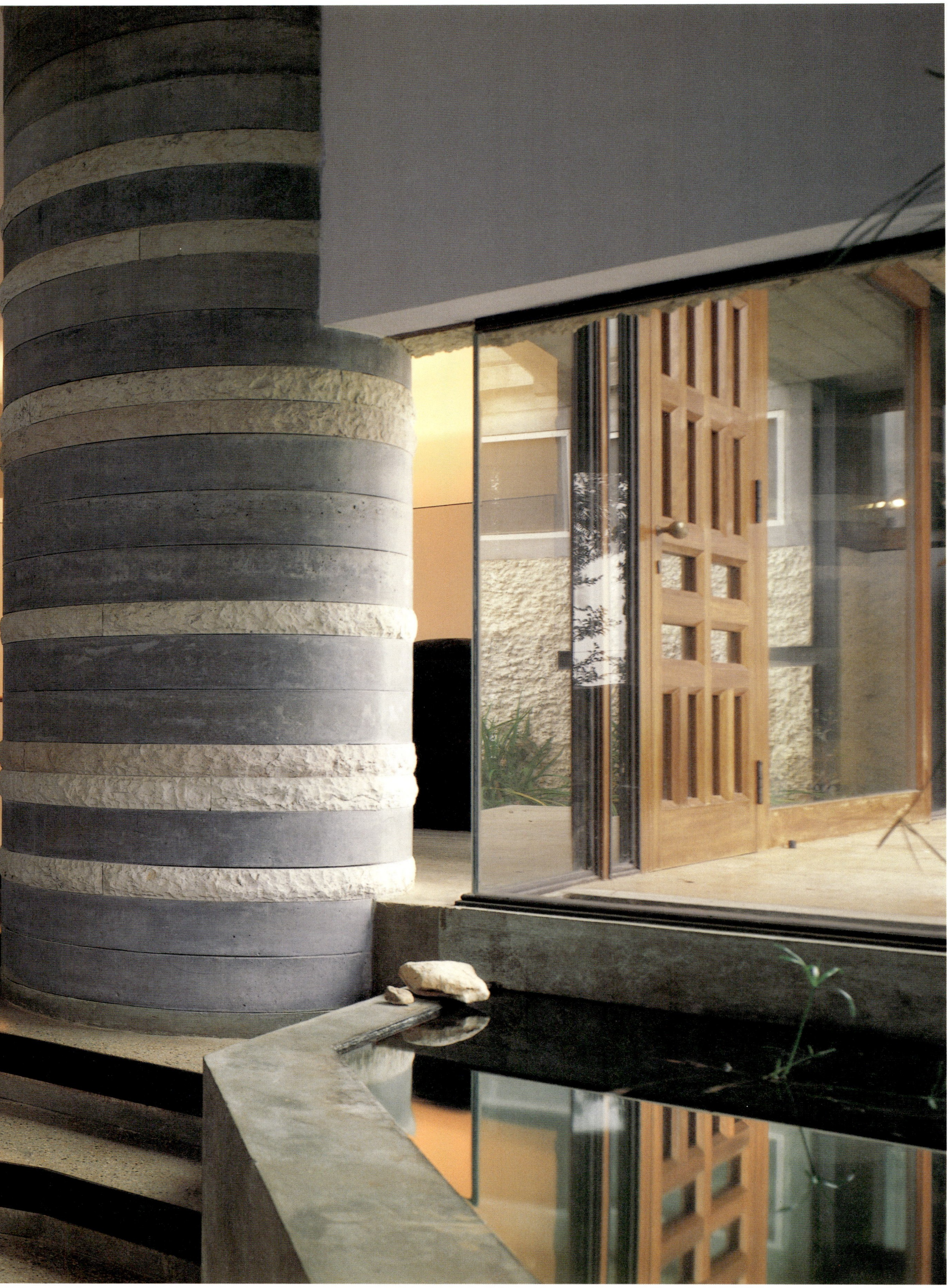

View toward master bedroom. Cylindrical volume for master bathroom

Master bedroom: master bathroom on right

68

View toward master bedroom from living room

Master bathroom

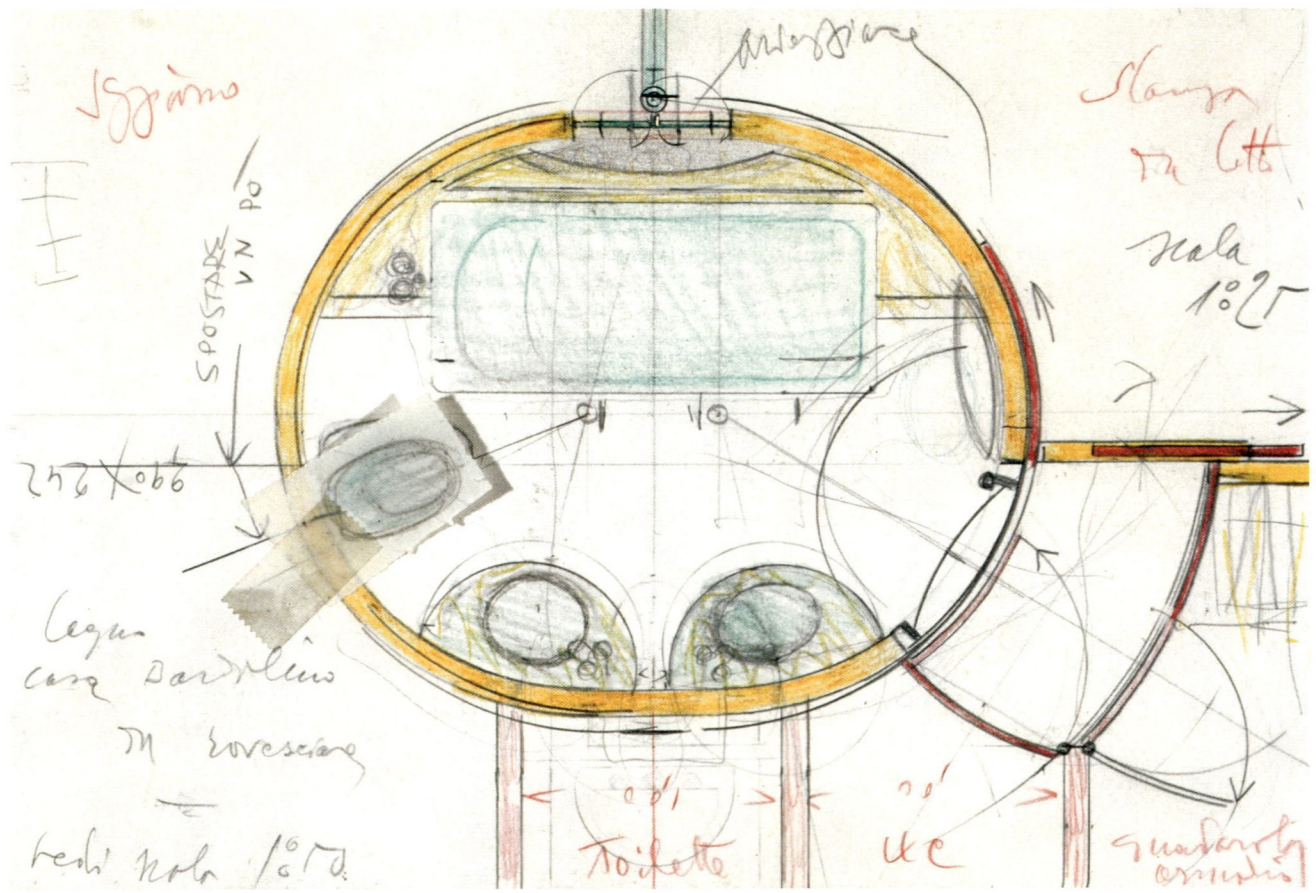

Plan: master bathroom

Master bedroom

世界現代住宅全集08
カルロ・スカルパ
ヴェリッティ邸
オットーレンギ邸

2010年11月25日発行
文：二川由夫
企画・編集・撮影：二川幸夫
アート・ディレクション：細谷巖
印刷・製本：大日本印刷株式会社
制作・発行：エーディーエー・エディタ・トーキョー
151-0051　東京都渋谷区千駄ヶ谷3-12-14
TEL.(03)3403-1581(代)

禁無断転載

ISBN 978-4-87140-633-8 C1352